Mobilization of the Church
Responding to God's Call for a Church of Action

By Nolan W. McCants

Mobilization of the Church
Copyright © 2002
by Nolan McCants

ISBN 1-931600-36-8

Published by
McCants Ministries
P.O. Box 9352
Naperville, IL 60567-9352
630.904.6262

www.mobilizationofthechurch.com

All rights reserved. No part of this book may be reproduced in any form without permission in writing from the publisher, except in the case of brief quotations embodied in critical articles or reviews.

All scripture quotations, unless otherwise indicated, are taken from the New King James Version. Copyright © 1982 by Thomas Nelson, Inc. Used by permission. All rights reserved.

Printed in the United States

Dedication

To my mother, Eleanor A. McCants,
for raising me in a home where Jesus was
acknowledged as Lord

Acknowledgments

My gratitude and special thanks to my loving wife Gloria, my children, Louis and his wife Daylena, and Joy and Staci for the sacrifices made for ministry to be expressed in this fashion.

To my Harvest Church Plainfield family for being a great people to serve with and a true representation of Christ in the earth.

A special thanks to Bishop Kirby and Sandra Clements for your motivation and support of my ministry. To April Bailey for editing this work *(here we are, in print again)*, Paul Phillips *(my mind reading design partner)* and to all of the hands that encouraged and touched this work.

Foreword

A prophetic note is quite evident in this work. A comparison between the contemporary church and the biblical pattern motivate the author to declare, not simply the need, but also some very significant solutions. Take note when you read this work, for it is a call to leaders and all the saints.

Bishop Kirby Clements
Cathedral at Chapel Hill

Introduction

As a child, I was blessed to be raised by a God-fearing woman who saw to it that my two brothers and I went to church. It was then that I came to know the Lord and immediately developed a real love for Him. It was as a teenager that I first developed a sense of what the corporate body of Jesus Christ was all about. Later in life, after years of building a public relations practice in Chicago, the Lord captured me and called me to plant a church in Plainfield, Illinois, a southwest suburb of Chicago. During the season that preceded this, God began to reveal to me the mystery of His body to a greater extent. This was a period of great hunger, and a series of humbling experiences pressed me into the presence of God. I mention this because I believe our greatest moments with God are very often our "lowest" moments in life.

During times of intimate prayer and study, God would show me the dysfunction in the body. I began to see with clarity how we had traded our real purpose as the church for religious tradition and empire building. As I began to look around and ask questions, it became clear to me that the church was experiencing an identity crisis. We have lost our identity and ceased to fully function as God intended. We have become immobilized, static and, in many instances, desperately ineffective. We are no longer functioning as salt and light. Sadly, it appears as though we've been more infected by the world than the world has been affected by us.

I do, however, believe that while this crisis exists, the prophetic words of Jesus shall not fall to the ground...

> *"And I also say to you that you are Peter, and on this rock I will build My church, and the gates of Hades shall not prevail against it."*
> Matthew 16:18 (NKJV)

This treatment of *Mobilization of the Church* is my first attempt at putting my thoughts in writing. I offer them as my gift to the Body. I hope they serve to offer encouragement, generate dialog, and cause the Body of Christ to revisit its God-ordained role in the earth today.

It's time for the *Mobilization of the Church!*

Mobilization of the Church
By Nolan W. McCants

Contents

	Introduction	
1.	Noah: A Symbol of Restoration	9
2.	The Church Defined by the Kingdom	19
3.	Thy Kingdom Come	23
4.	It Started in the Garden	26
5.	The Greater Commission	32
6.	The Multidimensional Church	38
7.	Equip and Release	44
8.	Motivation Not Stimulation	49
9.	Forming Strategic Alliances	53
10.	Secular and the Sacred	60
11.	The Clergy/Laity Dilemma	67
12.	The Measure of Our Success	73

1
Noah:
a Symbol of
Restoration

Then the LORD saw that the wickedness of man was great in the earth, and that every intent of the thoughts of his heart was only evil continually. And the LORD was sorry that He had made man on the earth, and He was grieved in His heart. So the LORD said, "I will destroy man whom I have created from the face of the earth, both man and beast, creeping thing and birds of the air, for I am sorry that I have made them." Genesis 6:5-7 (NKJV)

MOBILIZATION OF THE CHURCH

We are so blessed to have such treasures as those found in the Old Testament. Chronicled there are awesome accounts of God's moving which provide powerful insights into His ways, purposes and dealings with mankind. Noah, the subject of the story in Genesis 6, lived during a time when the depravity of man's heart so grieved God that it moved Him to bring to ruin all that had been His prized creation, including man, animal life and the earth.

God had warned Noah of the impending devastation that would soon engulf the whole earth, told him to build an ark, and followed with instructions on who and what should be brought into the ark for safekeeping.

> *"And behold, I Myself am bringing flood waters on the earth, to destroy from under heaven all flesh in which is the breath of life; everything that is on the earth shall die. "But I will establish My covenant with you; and you shall go into the ark; you, your sons, your wife, and your sons' wives with you. "And of every living thing of all flesh you shall bring*

> *two of every sort into the ark, to keep them alive with you; they shall be male and female. "Of the birds after their kind, of animals after their kind, and of every creeping thing of the earth after its kind, two of every kind will come to you to keep them alive. "And you shall take for yourself of all food that is eaten, and you shall gather it to yourself; and it shall be food for you and for them." Thus Noah did; according to all that God commanded him, so he did.* Genesis 6:17-22 (NKJV)

According to scripture, Noah, unlike the other inhabitants of the earth at that time, was just and walked blameless before God. As a result, he found grace in the eyes of the Lord. God does recognize and reward faithfulness and righteous living. In an effort to preserve a remnant representation of His righteousness in the earth, God told Noah to build an ark. You could consider it the world's first luxury cruise ship. I call it the quintessential Love Boat. Very explicit in every detail, the ark was God's chosen method of deliverance for Noah, his family and the other occupants of the vessel.

MOBILIZATION OF THE CHURCH

In this, Noah had been invited to walk in divine partnership with God. What a privilege and extraordinary opportunity. If only we would value and appreciate such opportunities today. We too have been included in the eternal plan of God, not just as active participants; we are covenant partners.

The story of Noah and his ark are most often related to the salvation of Noah's family and its correlation with our

> The ark was not intended to be the end, it was, in fact, a means to an end

deliverance as the redeemed people of God. But in developing the focus of this writing, let's consider the broader context.

While the story most certainly tells of God's plan of salvation for mankind, by following the story's progression, we also discover an even more amazing post-deliverance plan. Looking into this story, we can clearly see that Noah's ark was a shadow of the future church.

The ark was a symbol of hope for a bright and

glorious future, just as the church should be today. Every time we gaze into the sky at a rainbow, it serves as a reminder and perpetual expression of a promised hope.

First, I believe there is great significance in eight souls having been saved on the ark, (1 Peter 3:20). The number eight represents new beginnings, restoration, renewal, rebirth... a renaissance! For Noah, his family and even us today, this signified a fresh start with God.

In the traditional approach to this story, we stop at seeing the ark as a means of salvation alone. In doing so we miss the fullness of the story and the more immediate message to the church. The ark was not intended to be the end, it was, in fact, a means to an end. God had greater things in store for Noah and his traveling companions. In Jeremiah 29:11, the Lord states it this way...

> *"For I know the thoughts that I think toward you," says the LORD, "thoughts of peace and not of evil, to give you a future and a hope." (NKJV)*

MOBILIZATION OF THE CHURCH

God's plan extended far beyond salvation for Noah and his family. God in His infinite wisdom had simply included Noah in the orchestration of an extensive plan for the restoration of all things. Man, animals, plant life and even the earth itself was renewed during the flood. You should know that as obedient as Noah was, he could never have fathomed the significance and magnitude of his ministry. And for this reason, I stress to you that nothing you do for God should ever be minimized. Only God knows the extent of His working in and through us.

> *"For it is God who works in you both to will and to do for His good pleasure"*. Philippians 2:13 (NKJV).

There is a greater plan working in you today. Don't be limited by what you are able to see and measure.

It was immediately following the fall in the garden that we see God setting in motion His plan to regain all that was lost through the failure of Adam and Eve. God proclaimed,

> *"And I will put enmity between you and the woman, and between your seed and her Seed; He shall bruise your head, and you shall bruise His heel."* Genesis 3:15 (NKJV).

The Seed or offspring mentioned here speaks of the coming Christ who would do God's bidding on behalf of all mankind. The same seed was referenced in Galatians 3:16 (NKJV).

> *Now to Abraham and his Seed were the promises made. He does not say, "And to seeds," as of many, but as of one, "And to your Seed," who is Christ.*

As the body of Christ, this is so significant to the role of the Church in the earth today.

Secondly, it's important to note that God had not then, nor has He now, abandoned His original ideal. The flood was intended to do away with sin, not the eternal plan of God. The negative presentation of the gospel that we encounter all too often today would have us think that God's anger toward sin cancelled His plan for man. Nothing is farther from the truth.

MOBILIZATION OF THE CHURCH

On the contrary, God is yet operating with the thought of having a family of people who would elect of their own free will to worship Him, love him and personify Him in the earth. This powerful desire yet emanates from the heart of God, perhaps even more strongly today than ever before.

> ...we have the responsibility of bringing clarity and definition to what it means to be the church

The Bible says that Noah did according to all that the Lord had commanded him in Genesis 7:5. This highlights his obedience through faith. So Noah, his family, and the animals all entered the ark for their journey of faith as the waters began to rise. This became their season of transition, their process of redemption. It's what we experienced when we were brought out of darkness and delivered into His marvelous light, I Peter 2:9. But their story didn't end there and neither should ours.

Once the waters abated, Noah and his family left the ark. Immediately they approached the alter that Noah had erected. They brought forth burnt offerings and offered them to the Lord as a sign of their total submission. God then told Noah to release the animals and gave them the same directive that was given to the earth's's first animals as well as Adam and Eve in the garden.

> *So God blessed Noah and his sons, and said to them: "Be fruitful and multiply, and fill the earth. And the fear of you and the dread of you shall be on every beast of the earth, on every bird of the air, on all that move on the earth, and on all the fish of the sea. They are given into your hand."* Genesis 9:1-2 (NKJV)

Restoration is as much a part of the plan of salvation as salvation itself. Acts 3:20-21 says Jesus is being held in heaven until the restoration of all things. As the church, we've done well to address the need for salvation. The ark is overflowing with passengers. However, the concept of restoration has been relegated to some future event and narrowly defined as the supernatural work of the Holy Spirit.

MOBILIZATION OF THE CHURCH

Through the life of Noah, I believe it's clear that the church has a role to play here. I further believe we have the responsibility of bringing clarity and definition to what it means to be the church.

2
The Church Defined by the Kingdom

Anything that is misunderstood is bound to be abused. Mobilizing the church will first require a clear understanding of God's intent and design for the church. A basic understanding of the church is a prerequisite to accomplishing God's will.

Many people would assume that they already have a handle on God's intent for the church. But there are so many assumptions, most of which are born out of

MOBILIZATION OF THE CHURCH

culture and tradition. I have found that, for some, church is what we do on Sunday morning. For others, it's a beautifully adorned edifice complete with stained glass, a steeple and a choir loft. Then there are those who see the church as a private social club, where you must be grand fathered in to be accepted. For too many, it's the place they frequent on a weekly basis to get that fix that will enable them to go on just a little further. Sadly, their going on tends to be in pursuit of the things of this world rather than the will of God, but that's another sermon.

> ...our belief system or theology has left us with no impetus to progress

The prevailing thought in Christiandom is that the church's role is to simply get people saved, have them join our churches, become good Christians, and wait for Jesus to return so that we can all escape to heaven.

I believe this limited view of the church is one of the primary causes of our paralysis. We have become immobilized because our belief system or theology has left us with no impetus to progress.

MOBILIZATION OF THE CHURCH

It is true that doctrine produces an end product. In fact, it impregnates. This is why Jesus cautioned His disciples to be aware of the leaven or doctrine of the Pharisees. He knew that wrong doctrine would produce wrong actions.

This restricted view of the church has produced an attitude of indifference toward world affairs and the church's role in them. Jesus said that we are to be salt and light in the world in Matthew 5:13-14. We are to follow the pattern we've witnessed in His life during His earthly ministry. We should be compelled to do more than hide away behind the stained glass. We have been called to a purpose... and a very specific one.

A prerequisite to fully comprehending the purpose of the church is to understand the Kingdom of God. Because it is when we understand the "Kingdom and the Kingdom" agenda that true definition is given to the church. The term Kingdom of God speaks of the eternal rule and reign of God or another way of saying it is, the sovereign reign of Christ.

One of the problems we have here is that many have

MOBILIZATION OF THE CHURCH

commingled the two terms, referring to the church as the Kingdom and the Kingdom as the church. Thus the expression "build the Kingdom". We build the church, and the kingdom is progressively coming through this agent of redemption.

One primary distinction is that the church is finite, while the Kingdom is infinite. God's sovereignty was, is presently, and shall be in the future. The Kingdom is the ultimate end of God's plan and the church is a critical means to that end.

A fuller, more complete understanding of the Kingdom is vital to the mobilization of the church. I thank God there is a renewed interest in the subject of the Kingdom of God, and increased knowledge and revelation that's surfacing in the earth today because of it. Let us pray that His Kingdom would come and that His will would be done in the earth as it is in heaven. As it comes forth, the church will become more vibrant and clear to see in a dark world.

MOBILIZATION OF THE CHURCH

3
Thy Kingdom Come

Jesus spent His entire ministry talking about the Kingdom of God. He instructed us to pray for its coming, to seek it, and to enter it. This was so significant to Him that, after His resurrection, He spent 40 days prior to His ascension sharing with the disciples about the Kingdom. John the Baptist preceded Jesus, proclaiming that all should repent for the Kingdom was at hand. The Kingdom would appear in the embodiment of Jesus Himself.

The term itself has often been misunderstood and

misused. For years I was taught that it was simply heaven. In the parables when it was mentioned, it was viewed as either heaven or a future millennium kingdom.

I have since discovered that the Kingdom of God speaks of the rule and reign of Christ Jesus. An expansion of that concept would be the systems of heaven, the manner in which heaven operates. So when Jesus instructs His disciples to pray *thy Kingdom come*, He is essentially telling them to pray that heaven's systems would be the governing system in earth, just as it is in heaven. This governing is not some mysterious undertaking by the Holy Spirit. It begins with a very deliberate yielding of the individual to the systems of heaven, allowing an internal adjustment to take place. The church then becomes the corporate expression of this. The ultimate idea is for the church to then become salt and light in the world, infiltrating and influencing the systems of this world. In essence, while we are all waiting to go to heaven, we are called to bring heaven to earth.

Consider these distinctions. Many times we hear that

MOBILIZATION OF THE CHURCH

we are building the Kingdom, however the Kingdom is not built by us. The Kingdom, or God's rulership, is simply reestablished in the earth.

Again, the Kingdom was, is, and always will be. It is eternal, infinite. The church, on the other hand, is finite. It serves in a period that is situated between advents. It is the church that we are to build. It is primarily through the agency of the church that God re-establishes His Kingdom in the earth.

> It begins with a very deliberate yielding of the individual...

By further comprehending the Kingdom, it brings clarity to the present role and purpose of the church. It gives the church definition and provides for us an expanded and greater sense of purpose. When we preach or "walk out the Kingdom," we enunciate the rulership of God in every aspect of life. When we speak of the authority of Christ, we find in that healing, deliverance, prosperity, salvation and every other redemptive property.

So let's pray that His Kingdom would indeed come.

4
It Started in the Garden

It was in the garden of Eden that God gave Adam and Eve dominion and rulership over the earth. This was God's authority delegated to man for the purpose of overseeing and enjoying earthly matters. The couple was, in effect, made partners with God in the development and maintenance of God's prized creation. As they walked in obedience to Him, He faithfully provided everything they needed to achieve ultimate success.

God had in Adam a man filled with potential. He was also given the God-like power of choice. Adam had the potential for loving God or hating Him, pursuing Him or pursuing His creation. The choice to love would be walked out in Adam's life in the form of obedience and submission. It would be shown in his diligence to keep the garden and preserve the righteous ways of God. The authority of God over creation was wrapped up in the relationship He formed with Adam.

Because God would never violate His own decree, His access to Adam would be subject to Adam's will. It would also be Adam's choice to commune with God. There was no control, no dominance. God had not created puppets. Adam was a free agent, capable of making choices. And that he did to the detriment of us all.

A yielded, obedient Adam would have given God an earth-side agent, someone He could use who would work in concert with Him. Through regular communion with Adam, God could cast a reflection of Himself upon the earth. This consensual coming together gave God license to govern the steps of Adam and thus impact the world in which he lived.

MOBILIZATION OF THE CHURCH

It is this powerful concept of mutual submission that drives every meaningful relationship. It's called covenant. There is some debate surrounding the so-called Adamic covenant and that is not my argument here. My aim is only to highlight these awesome principles of covenant and how they determine the success or failure of the plans of God in our lives.

The fall of Adam and Eve meant the surrender of their delegated authority. They

> We must allow our view of the church to become stretched...

had been accessed by another. No longer exclusively governed by the creator of the heavens and the earth, they would now become the slave of the enemy and subject to a fallen nature. Thus, sin was left to run rampant throughout the earth and Satan then proceeded to establish his own kingdom or dominion.

He has fraudulently set up his kingdom of darkness through the manipulation of legitimate agencies such as the media, government, arts, entertainment, business, education, and even family. As a thief, he has robbed us of the beauty, benefit and purity found in these as was intended by God. Through these systems, the enemy has sought to pervert the wholeness and righteous purposes of God. They have been commandeered and used to defy God and destroy His creation. Where there is no Godly representation, God's access is limited in those areas.

Nevertheless, God has never ceased to be sovereign. He has never lost control. In the garden, at the fall of Adam and Eve, God immediately set in motion His plan to bring restoration to all things. His heart's intent would ultimately be fulfilled. What I find extraordinary about this plan is that God would still elect man, who had failed, to then defeat His enemy the devil. He didn't abandon His ideal, nor did He ever abandon us. His love never waned. He would forgive us in advance and then cut covenant through Abraham that would guarantee our success.

Through a series of covenants, God executed His plan. He enlists the partnership of Noah, Abraham, David, His Son Jesus Christ *(the second Adam),* and now the Church to achieve His eternal purposes. I call this final phase *"Operation Take Back."* And in the end, God will again reign supreme over all of heaven

MOBILIZATION OF THE CHURCH

and earth. In fact, the kingdoms of this world shall become His, fully and completely. (I Corinthians 15:24-28, Revelation 11:15)

Like Noah's ark, the church is God's chosen vehicle to deliver salvation. But not only salvation. Its design is such that not only is it capable of bringing salvation, it is also able to bring restoration. It is a container of the divine, equipped to fully restore that which was destroyed in the garden. Consider the significance of the cargo. Like the ark, the church contains cargo as well. In both the ark and the church, this cargo has reproductive qualities, giving it the ability to be fruitful, multiply, and replenish the earth with the righteous ways of God.

You must know that the Lord has never forgotten or abandoned His original idea of having a family of people who would worship Him and love His righteousness.

Adam was God's man in the earth and he enjoyed God's providential care. Through sin and rebellion, that authority and relationship was lost. But now, through an obedient second Adam, Jesus Christ, that authority has been reclaimed. All power in heaven and earth has become His. Now through His body, the church, this authority must now be actuated. The church has the capacity through the potency of the Holy Ghost to be fruitful and multiply, to subdue and have dominion. Much more than a saving station, the church is, in fact, an agent of redemption and restoration.

We must allow our view of the church to become stretched, expanded. More than just introducing people to Christ for the purpose of securing their eternal disposition, we must also impact the world in which we live. We must do well at what the first Adam failed miserably. Today, God is calling for a people who, through obedience and submission, will till His garden.

MOBILIZATION OF THE CHURCH

5
The Greater Commission

All too often, the so-called Great Commission of Matthew 28:19, has been perceived to be and sold as the lone function of the church. In the minds of many, this is the only mission with which the body has been charged. Such a restrictive view has resulted in the over-emphasis on evangelism at the expense of a fuller mandate.

The church is strong on bringing people into the knowledge of Christ, as it very well should be. However, where we have fallen short is in actually making disciples and in bringing people to a level of maturity that is required to become fully functioning, productive citizens of God's Kingdom. All of creation is awaiting the manifestation of such a body. (Romans 8:21)

Making disciples extends far beyond introducing people to the work of Christ and then just having them repeat the so-called Sinner's Prayer. The process of discipleship first requires a ready candidate, a person who is willing to lose his or her own life and take on the life of Christ. The word disciple means avid learner, student, follower of Christ. Unfortunately, discipleship has been reduced to the narrow definition of one who regularly goes to church. The well-equipped disciple will be brought into an understanding of what has transpired in their lives since having received Christ, the priorities of heaven, and what is expected of them.

> Making disciples extends far beyond introducing people to the work of Christ...

I believe this preoccupation with the end of time and the great Christian escape poses a real problem for the

MOBILIZATION OF THE CHURCH

church, as it too has immobilized us and even caused a withdrawal. The thought of flying away seems to have lessened the sense of urgency needed by the church today to respond to the priorities of heaven. One thing we know... the end *will* come. In the meantime, we are to occupy or do business.

With all of the hype surrounding being "left behind" you would think that this was most critical to God. Jesus never used fear to recruit disciples. He demonstrated a love that was in stark contrast to that of the world, a love that was attractive, yes, even irresistible. We must pour into people a truth that transforms and compels them to serve God with their whole heart.

The strategic placement of the church in the world is again part of a great redemptive and restorative plan. Until we hear something different from headquarters, we should ready the troops, encourage them, and lead them to the front lines of action.

MOBILIZATION OF THE CHURCH

How then should we be instructing our disciples?

We must first point them to the earthly life and ministry of Jesus Christ and the many powerful things that He modeled. His actions reveal the priorities of heaven and provide immediate direction to the church. As the body of Christ, we are to be the personification of His ministry.

> *"Most assuredly, I say to you, he who believes in Me, the works that I do he will do also; and greater works than these he will do, because I go to My Father.* John 14:12 (NKJV)

> *"For God so loved the world that He gave His only begotten Son, that whoever believes in Him should not perish but have everlasting life. For God did not send His Son into the world to condemn the world, but that the world through Him might be save."* John 3:16-17 (NKJV)

Consider the ways in which Christ related to the world.

- He related to sinners

- His response to the religious community was to dismantle their systems and demand adjustment, change, repentance

- He recruited His disciples out of the world and built genuine relationships with them

- He placed emphasis on being salt and light in and to the world

Making disciples means that people being discipled must be brought into a greater understanding of the reality of Christ living in them and all that it means. Teach them that they are no longer independent, but have become a part of the body of Christ. They are, in fact, in divine partnership with God. Therefore, it is critical that they learn to walk in covenant with God, their church and the universal body of Christ. They must be taught how to tap into the supernatural power of the Holy Spirit and the resources of heaven in order to fulfill their ultimate purpose in Christ. We should stress the importance of allowing the Holy Spirit to mold them and shape them into the image of Christ. Finally, they must understand that nothing can be achieved for the Kingdom without absolute obedience and wholehearted submission to our heavenly Father.

MOBILIZATION OF THE CHURCH

6
The Multidimensional Church

One of the most valid complaints lodged against the church in recent years is our having become irrelevant. We have perfected *having* church while failing miserably at *being* the church. We have failed to be salt and light in the critical areas.

Gone are the days of church being a building, Sunday school, morning worship, Easter service, Christmas service, and a few other regularly scheduled programs sprinkled throughout the year. The world is changing

MOBILIZATION OF THE CHURCH

and, as a consequence, the strategies of the church must change. People of this present world have needs that extend far beyond having membership in a warm, fuzzy neighborhood church. The demands of this life are forcing them to place a demand on the church that we cannot afford to ignore.

A successful church today must be multidimensional. It has to be prepared to minister to the entire person – body, soul, and spirit. There is such a hunger for fulfillment in life. People are searching for solutions to address a variety of needs in the areas of finance, family, relationships, marriage, parenting, health and career, in addition to things of the spirit.

> **We must press beyond the follow-the-leader mentality of replicating what we have seen others do**

While I am challenged by much of today's perverted teachings on prosperity, I understand clearly why people flock in droves to this teaching. There is a cry for instruction on how to live life and how to live it God's way... abundantly. Even psychics are being

MOBILIZATION OF THE CHURCH

visited by more than a few unenlightened Christians looking for answers. As the church of the 21st century, we have a responsibility to break from our traditions, invite a paradigm shift, and become comprehensive in our approach to ministry. I'm not in any way suggesting we respond to the world's cry for more. I'm saying, in God there are legitimate solutions – *practical and supernatural* – to legitimate problems. We simply need to uncover those solutions in God's Word and seek creative ways to bring them to the attention of the world.

The multidimensional church will seek to understand the widening needs of both their faith community as well as the larger community outside its walls, and then look for creative ways to address them. Now, understandably, none can be all things to all men, but we can certainly be more things to some men. Partnering with other ministries that have strengths in specific areas can also aid in your ministry reach.

We must be open to doing things a bit differently than we have in the past. We must press beyond the follow-the-leader mentality of replicating what we have seen others do. The multidimensional church

MOBILIZATION OF THE CHURCH

will have depth, it will create new paradigms, new expanded ways of doing ministry. It will challenge itself to escape the norms.

One of the areas that I believe must be challenged in our thinking is the whole concept of clergy and laity. The hierarchal order places a few good men and women at the top and the rest of the folks at the bottom. The idea is that those at the top know everything, do everything and are everything. The congregation, being the other folks, simply observes this process from the safety of their pews and tap in whenever a certain need arises. This lifeless concept is as far from the biblical model of the church as we can get it. I'll deal with this subject is greater detail in a subsequent chapter.

I am fully convinced that there is so much untapped creativity seated in pews all over the world. The greatest challenge now is that we have successfully conditioned people to think this way. As a result, they come and they sit and they may initially be offended if asked to do any more.

So there is a need for reformation, a re-forming of our

MOBILIZATION OF THE CHURCH

thinking about ministry, a collective reforming of ideas about church and what God's intent is for the church. A reforming from the top to the bottom. Reform is the true meaning of repentance, by the way. Most of us folk at the top get real nervous when the message of repentance visits the doors of our religious systems.

The first step to becoming a multidimensional church is to look around and see the obvious. There are needs. Don't be afraid to fail at trying something new or different to meet those needs. Take the plunge and allow others around you to try and fail as well. Failure is a critical ingredient to any success. Ask lots of questions of those around you and press others to do the same. Most of all, continue to ask yourself why you do what you do at every level and then don't be afraid to change something once it's been discovered that it has outlived its usefulness or never made a lot of sense in the first place. Close that religious gap between the so-called clergy and laity. We have been called to empower people and equip them to do ministry. Jesus cautioned that we were never to lord it over people.

MOBILIZATION OF THE CHURCH

Pray and ask the Lord to unleash the creativity that's presently within your faith community. I believe new ideas will flow like a river, your church will become vibrant, viable, and lives will begin to be changed within and outside the walls of the church.

7
Equip and Release

> *Then God blessed them, and God said to them, "Be fruitful and multiply; fill the earth and subdue it; have dominion over the fish of the sea, over the birds of the air, and over every living thing that moves on the earth."*
> Genesis 1:28 (NKJV)

Man has built into his very nature the desire and capacity to engage in productive and meaningful activity. We have all been given certain gifts and talents that need to be identified, maximized and

MOBILIZATION OF THE CHURCH

utilized. I contend that much of the senseless wranglings that go on in many churches is because there is no real infrastructure in place to provide for this sort of development and release. We're stuck in the pyramid. Those at the top do all, those at the bottom watch.

God created us all to be doers, to be productive citizens of His Kingdom. In our secular jobs and volunteer organizations, there are systems in place to develop and then mobilize those who sign on to be a part of the unfolding of their dreams. The church must do no less. We must begin to evaluate our systems and make adjustments where necessary to make sure we have created environments conducive to equipping and releasing.

> In their seemingly defiant way, most people are screaming out, let me do what I was made to

MOBILIZATION OF THE CHURCH

Releasing

We must go beyond seeing the church as a place for gathering only. There must be a deliberate plan in place to release those gifts that are in the house. Just as Jesus did with his disciples, we must recognize them, embrace them, affirm them, and then release them.

> *Then He said to them, "The harvest truly is great, but the laborers are few; therefore pray the Lord of the harvest to send out laborers into His harvest."* Luke 10:2 (NKJV)

It is my sincere belief that many of the challenges we've encountered with church hoppers, over-zealous attention-seekers, complainers and the like, is the frustration that occurs when we fail to put them to work. Of course, there are always the mavericks who will resist authority at any cost.

In their seemingly defiant way, most people are screaming out, let me do what I was made to do. Let me lead a life of productivity. To compound the problem, most of these people are regularly affirmed

MOBILIZATION OF THE CHURCH

and put to work in their secular work places. The problem has been that the church has been extremely limited in the kinds of opportunities we've created for people.

These limitations are the product of our inward focus. Our idea of work is serving on some committee, ministry or board as it relates to the internal operation of the church. Here is where we must strive to think outside of the box. We need to call upon the Lord for a fresh impartation of creativity and for a clearer view of the church's role outside of the box. It's time for new paradigms. We've played follow the leader far too long.

The world we live in is much different than that of our parents. There are limitless opportunities to influence and infiltrate world systems. The Internet, as one example, is so ripe for ministry. Most churches, if they even have a website, tend to have static sites – uninteresting, repetitive information about service times, location, and bios on key leaders. Through this technology, churches can webcast Bible studies utilizing streamed audio and video. Information can be disseminated for meetings,

MOBILIZATION OF THE CHURCH

worker's supports, and volunteer training. Chat rooms can be created to prompt dialog on just about any topic. The possibilities are endless. In many cases, it's just a matter of adjusting some priorities.

In every ministry there needs to be a team comprised of a cross-section of people representing the various ages, sexes, and cultures of our communities. They could be assembled to hold periodic brainstorming sessions for the express purpose of developing new models and new paradigms. Another interconnected group could be tasked with identifying the various giftings that may be present in the house, and then connecting them with functioning or developing ministries where there might be a fit.

It's not enough to get people saved. We must complete the process of equipping them with knowledge and understanding about the fuller purposes of God, aid in identifying what God has deposited within them, create an environment within which they can be developed, and then release them with the expectation of their becoming productive citizens of God's Kingdom.

8
Motivation Not Stimulation

There has been enough stimulation in the body of Christ to go around. Stimulation, defined here, is the external, or fleshly urging of people to respond to the work of ministry. It is the employment of gimmickry and other tactics to provoke a specific response. Stimulation in this sense only produces emptiness in the people, and a need on the part of the leader to continue to prime the pump. What true incentive can we offer people to express true worship toward God in a selfless and loving way? How can we motivate the people of God?

MOBILIZATION OF THE CHURCH

To motivate is to provide a motive, a reason for doing what needs to be done. Motivation will occur when the complete message of the gospel is made clear in a healthy environment, free of gimmickry and groundless promises.

Motivating the people of God can be difficult and for a variety of reasons. Many Christians have simply not allowed themselves to be transformed by the renewing of their minds. They have accepted Christ, but they yet think and process life through a worldly paradigm. They must continue to hear a Word that will aid in their being transformed. Others have been raised on what I call "hyper-gospel." This is a presentation of the gospel that makes big promises of joy, happiness, and prosperity sans the need for covenant and self-sacrifice.

> To motivate is to provide a motive, a reason for doing...

There are a number of things that I believe motivate people to touch ministry:

1. A real encounter with God
2. An understanding of what happened when they came to Christ
3. An understanding of the heaven's present focus as it relates to the Kingdom of God
4. Models of ministry in action
5. Models of integrity *(ministry that produces what it preaches)*
6. A covenant mentality
7. A true love and appreciation for what God has done in their lives

It will require patience to instruct and provide loving guidance to those we serve. Constant reminders of God moving must be illustrated through the Word and in present-day demonstration. In every possible way, we must point people to the fruit of ministry, fruit that can be seen in attitudes reshaped as well as lives and communities changed. There must be the evidence of meaningful ministry that is produced through our

MOBILIZATION OF THE CHURCH

churches today. And if there is an absence of such activity, we must go to God and inquire of Him.

We should probably take a look at our annual church calendars to see what fills them. Many times it's the redundant lifeless "church" activities that clog up church calendars. These activities have proven to be a source of pleasure for a few congregational diehards and sheer boredom for the majority. Such activities tend to be tremendous morale killers. While most people may not complain, don't let that fool you. They will cast their vote through their lack of participation or financial support. It may not always mean a cutting away. It might just be wise to cut back. Reducing the frequency of such events, refocusing, and reprioritizing may breathe new life into your church. As always, a few may be displeased, but pruning is needful and beneficial in the long term.

The church needs creativity and strategy that will impact the world in which we live. After all, the God we serve is THE creator. When people are witnesses to the mighty hand of God moving in the lives of people and the world around them, they will become motivated.

9
Forming Strategic Alliances

(...He who descended is also the One who ascended far above all the heavens, that He might fill all things.) And He Himself gave some to be apostles, some prophets, some evangelists, and some pastors and teachers, for the equipping of the saints for the work of ministry, for the edifying of the body of Christ, till we all come to the unity of the faith and of the knowledge of the Son of God, to a perfect man, to the measure of the stature of the fullness of Christ. Ephesians 4:10-13

MOBILIZATION OF THE CHURCH

When the church is mentioned in scripture, it may not yet have occurred to many that it wasn't referring to their local church. In scripture, the mention of the church was in reference to the universal body of Jesus Christ.

The healthiest view that can be maintained is that of the corporate body of Jesus Christ. Building the church is far more than building our individual ministries. In fact, that position is a very dangerous and self-defeating posture. The gifting that Christ deposited into the body was not to be isolated and confined to a single church or organization.

While we are all equipped with certain gifts, none of us possess every gift. It's important to remain open to relationships with others having complimentary gifts. Recognizing that you cannot do ministry as an autonomous part of the body is extremely important.

What we do must always be in light of the universal body of Christ. Our building is part part of a much greater eternal strategy, greater than us, greater than our local churches and, yes, even greater than our denomination or network. A localized mind set is

MOBILIZATION OF THE CHURCH

very limiting and very much against the plan of God for His church.

We are all aware of our strong sides and our weak sides. We can either pretend our weak sides are nonexistent and erect walls of pride to insulate ourselves, or we can acknowledge them and then seek out the relationships and resources that can aid in our becoming more complete. It is vitally important to establish early how we will respond to the ever-unfolding revelation of who we are not.

> **It is vitally important to establish early how we will respond to the ever-unfolding revelation of who we are not**

Forming strategic alliances within the Body of Christ can be so beneficial, in fact, mutually beneficial for those open to growth and those accepting the challenge to move beyond their comfort zones.

> *Two are better than one, because they have a good reward for their labor. For if they fall, one will lift up his companion. But woe to him*

> *who is alone when he falls, for he has no one to help him up. Again, if two lie down together, they will keep warm; but how can one be warm alone? Though one may be overpowered by another, two can withstand him. And a threefold cord is not quickly broken.* Ecclesiastes 4:9-12 (NKJV)

More than a good idea, it is a God idea. He has so wonderfully gifted each individual and then given us to one another. We must now learn to appreciate one another and go another step and seek out meaningful relationships.

It is important to develop a mix of relationships that include:

Non-believers
People of varied cultures
People located in different geographic locales
Peers and elders
Ministers from various denominations
Community leaders

Business professionals
Local government officials
Representatives of the local media

Breaking down the barriers

There are a number of hindrances to forming alliances and building valuable relationships. These can be summed up in one word – insecurity. It is the fear that we will either be tainted by another or that we will be exposed as being the flawed, deficient people we really are. I'm afraid that all too often we buy into our own public personas. Forming alliances will first demand a level of vulnerability that most aren't willing to chance because it means exposing their weak side. There is so much to be gained if we could only put legs to this idea.

MOBILIZATION OF THE CHURCH

I believe the most common and most damning barriers are listed below:

- Differing theology
- Race and culture
- Fear of being hurt
- Pride
- Ignorance
- Self sufficiency
- Refusal to explore
- Narrow definition of Christianity

We must be deliberate in our effort to overcome these, reach across those invisible boundaries and be broadened. At any cost, we must be determined to break down the barriers that have divided.

The remedy begins with open and honest dialog. We must get to know one another and seek to discover those things that we agree on. We can begin with short-term projects that allow for the equal participation of all involved and an opportunity for each to contribute from their strong side, and willingly give way to others to fill in the blanks of

MOBILIZATION OF THE CHURCH

their weak side. Once the door of opportunity has opened, you will first discover that while your journeys have been different, the challenges faced along the way were very similar. This makes for a sure "love connection" and creates the platform for building a lasting, more meaningful relationship.

Some final notes... Never feel that every relationship has to be the same. You'll need brothers, sisters, mothers and fathers in the faith. There will be some with whom there will be immediate chemistry, while other relationships will have to be nurtured. Additionally, relationships vary in duration and regularity of contact. Go with the flow, choose to see the good and put the unfavorable you may encounter in people in perspective. We're all in process. Let love be the governing principal and patience sustain you as you build. In building remember, covenant is mutual and requires death to take effect.

10
Secular and the Sacred

What place does the church serve in society? How are we to relate to this present world? Where are the boundaries and who created them? These are questions the church needs to ponder and create dialog around as we consider the present role of the church in the world.

Pseudo lines have been drawn creating a distinction between what has become known as the sacred and the secular. These are lines drawn to prescribe for the church the safe areas of her operation and influence. It suggests a clearly defined division.

MOBILIZATION OF THE CHURCH

Basically, these lines restrict the church to its hollowed edifices on Sundays and allow only token religious participation in the real world, so to speak. Sadly, it's not clear whether this attitude was derived from the world or from within the church. My sneaking suspicion is that it is the manufacture of religious systems, systems that must come down if we are ever to become effective as the church. I also believe it is another case where the church has been influenced by world systems as opposed to the converse occurring.

Look at Isaiah 66:1-2...

> *Thus says the LORD: "Heaven is My throne, and earth is My footstool. Where is the house that you will build Me? And where is the place of My rest? For all those things My hand has made, and all those things exist," says the LORD. "But on this one will I look: on him who is poor and of a contrite spirit, and who trembles at My word."*
>
> The Psalmist writes...*The earth is the Lord's, and all its fullness, the world and those who*

MOBILIZATION OF THE CHURCH

> *dwell therein.* Psalms 24:1 (NKJV)

There are no boundaries that restrict God. He goes where He wants and touches whomever and whatever He desires. As His representatives, we must not harbor any fear or reservations about going to all the world and ministering the gospel of the kingdom. Jesus said...

> *"Go into all the world and preach the gospel to every creature."* Mark 16:15 (NKJV)

The most prevailing attitude of "touch-not, taste-not, handle-not" must be adjusted to come into alignment with the earthly ministry of Jesus. Consider this pre-departure prayer of Jesus and some of the relationships He pursued that are highlighted in the gospels. What is the message that these send to the church?

> *"I do not pray that You should take them out of the world, but that You should keep them from the evil one. "They are not of the world, just as I am not of the world. "Sanctify them by Your truth. Your word is truth. "As You*

MOBILIZATION OF THE CHURCH

sent Me into the world, I also have sent them into the world. "And for their sakes I sanctify Myself, that they also may be sanctified by the truth. "I do not pray for these alone, but also for those who will believe in Me through their word; "that they all may be one, as You, Father, are in Me, and I in You; that they also may be one in Us, that the world may believe that You sent Me. "And the glory which You gave Me I have given them, that they may be one just as We are one:"I in them, and You in Me; that they may be made perfect in one, and that the world may know that You have sent Me, and have loved them as You have loved Me."Father, I desire that they also whom You gave Me may be with Me where I am, that they may behold My glory which You have given Me; for You loved Me before the foundation of the world."O righteous Father! The world has not known You, but I have known You; and these have known that You sent Me."And I have declared to them Your name, and will declare it, that the love with which You loved Me may be in them, and I in them." John 17:15-26 (NKJV)

Risky Business

Jesus regularly tread upon what we would call secular soil to influence the lives of those He'd sought to save. He broke all of our sacred rules today and crossed every secular line there was to cross, so much so that He was called a glutton and a drunkard, a friend of tax collectors and sinners! (Luke 7:34) In fact, His very first recorded miracle was turning water into wine at a wedding party.

Two of my favorite stories are about Matthew the tax collector and little Zacchaeus, a publican and tax collector. I particularly fancy Zacchaeus, as I can personally relate to his short stature. Here are two

> ...we are too concerned with our image and our reputation among others like us

men of the world who had heard about this Jesus. Because of their professions, neither were probably known for their integrity. Tax collectors had a reputation for taking bribes and adding a little juice to the taxes to line their own pockets.

MOBILIZATION OF THE CHURCH

The thing that struck me most about the relationship that Jesus formed with these worldly people is that he did not shun them, nor did he invite them to come into His world. To the contrary, he graciously invited Himself into theirs. He never feared going on their turf, as we modern Christians have been known to express. In neither story did there seem to be a rush on Jesus' part to meet an agenda. He simply focused on building a genuine relationship and acting as a true friend, a friend to sinners, no less. What a simple but powerful demonstration of who God really wants to be and desires that we would be to the world.

Unfortunately, we are too concerned with our image and our reputation among others like us. Why, how would it look if we were caught associating with the likes of Zacchaeus or Matthew? And yet, we ask why it's so difficult to reach family members, friends, and co-workers. The problem is that we're playing by the wrong set of rules. The church must free itself from these false restrictions and go where it's needed most – in the world where we were sent.

MOBILIZATION OF THE CHURCH

Read this popular passage in light of Jesus' actions.

> *"For God so loved the world that He gave His only begotten Son, that whoever believes in Him should not perish but have everlasting life.* John 3:16 (NKJV)

Let's do away with the lines that have confined the church, and seek God for creative strategies to infiltrate the world and advance the authority of God's Kingdom. It's time we become mobilized, going into all the world to minister life without fear or reservation.

11
The Clergy/Laity Dilemma

The division of clergy, those who supposedly play a more important role in the execution of the plan of God, and laity, those having a lesser responsibility, has aided in immobilizing the body. Paul writes,

> *For as the body is one and has many members, but all the members of that one body, being many, are one body, so also is Christ. For by one Spirit we were all baptized into one body; whether Jews or Greeks, whether slaves or free; and have all been*

MOBILIZATION OF THE CHURCH

made to drink into one Spirit. For in fact the body is not one member but many. If the foot should say, "Because I am not a hand, I am not of the body," is it therefore not of the body? And if the ear should say, "Because I am not an eye, I am not of the body," is it therefore not of the body? If the whole body were an eye, where would be the hearing? If the whole were hearing, where would be the smelling? But now God has set the members, each one of them, in the body just as He pleased. And if they were all one member, where would the body be? But now indeed there are many members, yet one body. And the eye cannot say to the hand, "I have no need of you"; nor again the head to the feet, "I have no need of you." No, much rather, those members of the body which seem to be weaker are necessary. And those members of the body which we think to be less honorable, on these we bestow greater honor; and our unpresentable parts have greater modesty, but our presentable parts have no need. But God composed the body, having given greater honor to that part which lacks it, that there

MOBILIZATION OF THE CHURCH

> *should be no schism in the body, but that the members should have the same care for one another.* 1 Corinthians 12:12-25 (NKJV)

It is by the grace of God alone that we have differing roles. Nevertheless, we all share equally in carrying out the purposes of God. The church's role is to equip, not Lord over people. Rather than create a congregation of dependent churchgoers who feel the necessity to return week after week to get their fix, Jesus gave the mandate to make disciples – avid, disciplined learners who would take up their crosses and follow Jesus, not our denominations, churches or pet doctrine.

Now this is not to suggest that there are no governing authorities in the body. We serve a God of order and there is no doubt that order is essential to productivity. Submission and obedience to those serving in these capacities will please the Father and dramatically enhance our potential for success. This is so powerfully demonstrated in the relationship between the Father, the Son, and the Holy Spirit.

However, even in this, it is important that we view

this authority from a kingdom perspective. The word authority in the New Testament comes from the Greek word *exousia,* which has

> ...we all share equally in carrying out the purposes of God

to do with delegated influence. Husbands, parents, pastors, and teachers have all been strategically placed in the lives of others to influence their producing fruit that will bring glory to our Heavenly Father.

The whole idea of clergy and laity incorrectly brings the priestly concept of the Old Testament over into the church age. In the Old Testament, it was the priests alone who would represent the people before God, receive direction from God, and initiate worship in presenting the various sacrifices.

> *And Jesus cried out with a loud voice, and breathed His last. Then the veil of the temple was torn in two from top to bottom.* Mark 15:37-38 (NKJV).

MOBILIZATION OF THE CHURCH

At this moment all was changed. The veil that was once restricted to the priests of old was now open and available to all who came in the name of the Lord. Paul writes,

> *"But you are a chosen generation, a royal priesthood, a holy nation, His own special people, that you may proclaim the praises of Him who called you out of darkness into His marvelous light."* 1 Peter 2:9 (NKJV)

Today, it is the responsibility of every believer to enter into the presence of God and develop a meaningful relationship with Him. No priest, pastor or parent can stand before God for us. We have an individual responsibility to visit with God and seek His direction for our lives and ministry. Our personal worship can't be reiterated enough. This should be expressed in our lifestyles, attitudes, and service. Every believer must be taught the depth of their part in God's eternal plan and challenged to take ownership of this priestly obligation.

Those serving in places of influence have tried for many generations to serve in this dual capacity.

MOBILIZATION OF THE CHURCH

Unfortunately, all that has been accomplished is many great leaders suffering burnout and a people that have yet to be fully empowered or mobilized.

12
The Measure of Our Success
A note to leaders in the Body of Christ

Success in the Kingdom of God isn't the same as success in the world. And whenever we try to apply worldly measures of success to ministry, frustration, and a sense of defeat follows. If Gideon had used the measuring rod of the world, he would never have been able to follow God.

To effectively move people forward, we must first be clear on the priorities of heaven. What's important to God? Is it buildings, grand ordinations, anniversary celebrations, baby dedications or drawing large crowds? We must know what is critical to God generally and specifically, and be about the business of bringing that to pass.

There is something about time that can cause us to lose sight of these priorities, and we can then easily find ourselves drifting off course. Once this happens, we begin to measure our success by the roar of the crowd or the volume of activity, rather than by what pleases God. In scripture, there were many who were simply called to warn the people without having any expectancy of a response to the Word of the Lord.

We must first be clear on heaven's goals and objectives, and have a vision of how these apply to our own ministries. There has to be a commitment made to these priorities, a determination that says I won't be swayed or distracted by the lessor things of this world. You must write these priorities out in language that the entire church can comprehend and make applicable to their own areas of ministry and lives. Your values and their values must be consistent with God's values. Regularly revisit these in preaching, teaching, publications, staff and volunteer

MOBILIZATION OF THE CHURCH

meetings, and don't forget to remind yourself.

Anxiety and frustration borne out of the process of ministry can cause us to wander. We must periodically step back from our labors and take an honest look at what we're doing. Now, whenever you do this, never go in counting. It's not always in the numbers. I have discovered that God places His hand on consistency of obedience and the pursuit of His master plan. In assessing, you simply want to be able to determine whether you are staying the course with what God has delivered to you or drifting into wanting to see measurable results that do not necessarily correspond to the pre-determined goals and objectives of heaven.

> ...God places His hand on consistency of obedience...

Make it clear to the people who serve alongside you that you are determined to pursue the priorities of heaven. This will mean making some difficult decisions and vetoing a few as well. And even in this, you will make mistakes and some wrong decisions. Don't be held captive to your mistakes and don't let

MOBILIZATION OF THE CHURCH

people bind you by them. Remember, you're not in a popularity contest. You only need the esteem of one voice, your heavenly Father.

Churches are made up of people from all walks of Christian life. If you have a person or persons around you who have a different view of what spells success, they can potentially influence you to take alternate routes. I encourage you to stick with the plan. Lead with wisdom and grace. Taking a position can be done without coming off as dictatorial. Work to build relationships, share your thoughts and vision as God has given it to you. This will help to bring them around to seeing what you see and how you see it.

As you move forward, there will be the need to modify or make adjustments as God gives more revelation and more clarity to your specific purpose in His universal plan. Go with His flow and don't be afraid to make changes. This is the downfall of many who are fearful and afraid to follow God as His tactics and strategies change for their ministry.

Finally, celebrate your successes. Bring it to the attention of your church when you have achieved

MOBILIZATION OF THE CHURCH

something that lines up with the plan. Be vigilant, intentional and deliberate in your actions. And never, never apologize for following the plan of the most high God. Undergird all that you do with prayer. It is essential that you maintain regular contact with headquarters. With this, you will achieve true success. With this, you will *Mobilize the Church.*

Amen!

The Author

Nolan W. McCants is known as a leader of leaders and has a real heart for aiding men and women in discovering their purpose in God and becoming all that God would have them to be. Professionally, McCants was owner of a full-service public relations firm which handled Fortune 50 corporations, non-for-profit agencies, entrepreneurs and entertainment clients.

McCants does well to translate the Bible's stated purpose for the church into practical terms. His insightful, humorous, dynamic and charismatic speaking style combines both his experience as an entrepreneur and pastor to inspire, stimulate thought and motivate others to act on behalf of the Kingdom.

Nolan is married to Gloria, his wife of 19 years. Together they founded Harvest Church Plainfield, in Plainfield, Illinois, a southwest suburb of Chicago. They have three children.

MOBILIZATION OF THE CHURCH

Published by
McCants Ministries
P.O. Box 9352
Naperville, IL 60567-9352
630.904.6262
www.mccantsministries.com

Cover Concept: Nolan McCants
Graphic Illustration: Paul Phillips

Contact us for bulk order discounts